DATE DUE		

92
HUB

43442
Datnow, Claire L.

Edwin Hubble :
discoverer of
galaxies

WINFIELD PUBLIC SCHOOL
WINFIELD, IL. 60190

870720 02395   37389B   0001

Great Minds of Science

Edwin Hubble

Discoverer of Galaxies

Revised Edition

Claire L. Datnow

Enslow Publishers, Inc.
40 Industrial Road
Box 398
Berkeley Heights, NJ 07922
USA

http://www.enslow.com

Acknowledgments

The author would like to thank Kurt Bachman, assistant professor at Birmingham Southern College, for technical assistance, and Jennie Stevens for assistance with editing the book. I would also like to thank my husband Boris Datnow for his ongoing critique and support.

Library of Congress Cataloging-in-Publication Data

Datnow, Claire L.
    Edwin Hubble : discoverer of galaxies / Claire L. Datnow. — [Rev. ed.].
        p. cm. — (Great minds of science)
    Includes bibliographical references and index.
    ISBN-13: 978-0-7660-2791-6
    ISBN-10: 0-7660-2791-0
    1. Hubble, Edwin Powell, 1889–1953—Juvenile literature.
    2. Astronomers—United States—Biography—Juvenile literature.
    [1. Hubble, Edwin Powell, 1889–1953. 2. Astronomers.] I. Title.
    QB36.H83D38 2007
    520.92—dc22
    [B]
                                                    2006020111

Printed in the United States of America

10 9 8 7 6 5 4 3 2 1

Illustration Credits: AP/Wide World Photos, pp. 60, 66, 75, 101; copyright © Carnegie Institution of Washington, pp. 6, 38, 58, 93; Huntington Library, pp. 14, 15, 18, 23, 39, 44, 50, 62, 85, 87, 97; Jupiterimages Corporation, p. 105; Yerkes Observatory Photographs, pp. 20, 30, 33, 79.

Cover Illustration: Yerkes Observatory Photographs (foreground); NASA (background).

Contents

Introduction: Hubble's Quest

ON CHRISTMAS EVE, 1919, THE YOUNG astronomer Edwin Hubble got ready to work through the long cold night at the Mount Wilson Observatory. The observatory stood high on a mountaintop 5,714 feet above the city of Pasadena, California. The observatory housed the giant 100-inch Hooker telescope, then the most powerful in the world. Though far away from family and friends, Hubble was getting his first chance to use the telescope. With this tool he would see objects in the night sky more clearly than ever before, and might even discover never-before-seen stars.

He put on his heavy, winter army coat, then climbed the steep flight of iron stairs to the observing platform. On the platform, a cold wind whipped the coat around his tall frame.[1] Through a slit in the observatory's giant dome, stars

Edwin Hubble spent many sleepless nights peering out into space. His hard work and dedication would make him one of the most famous astronomers of all time.

glittered in the black sky. On the floor below, his night assistant, Milton Humason, waited at the control panel. The dim light from the panel cast a red glow over the area.

When Hubble gave the signal, Humason pushed the buttons on the control panel to start the electric motors. The motors set three different parts of the observatory moving at once—the platform, dome, and telescope. The observing platform on which the astronomers stood rose and rotated. At the same time the dome, attached to wheels and a track, slowly revolved in the opposite direction. When the dome was in place, Humason needed to adjust the slit so that the light from the star Hubble wanted to observe that night shone directly on the telescope's mirror.

With a series of clicks Hubble locked the telescope onto its target. If necessary, Humason could raise the platform a little higher so that Hubble could better reach the eyepiece of the telescope. With everything in place, Edwin Hubble bent low and looked through the eyepiece. The telescope made a nebula thousands of light-years away look close enough to reach out and touch.

With his fingers and thumb on the controls of the huge telescope, Hubble could begin a voyage through space. He began photographing the night sky. This could be a tricky process. The telescope had to follow the stars moving across the sky without losing sight of them. To do this, Hubble stood with his eye fixed to the eyepiece of the telescope while he adjusted the controls to keep track of the stars. At the same time, the dome's slit had to be adjusted to stay open in front of the telescope's mirror.

This telescope was the greatest gift any astronomer could have wished for. Its 100-inch polished mirror made objects light-years away from the earth visible. The extra-powerful telescope could take the clearest photographs of nebulae ever made. Before this, other astronomers had seen them only as faintly glowing smudges in the sky.

Through the night Hubble had to focus on taking the best possible photographs. Even when tired, sleepy, and cold, he had to keep his hands steady. This was not easy. The bitter cold mountain air numbed his fingers and toes.

In those days astronomers did not have the use of powerful computers. Unlike astronomers today, Hubble did not sit inside a heated room at a computer keyboard. He did his work exposed to the mountain air. With no high-tech computers to assist him, he had to stay alert.

At midnight the astronomer could take a break in an unheated concrete bunker under the telescope. There he stretched his cramped muscles. To renew his energy he chewed on hard biscuits and sipped on a steaming mug of cocoa. Then he climbed back up to the telescope platform to continue his work.

At dawn the light from the sun dimmed the stars. His work was over for the night. Hubble made his way down a narrow path along the mountaintop. After bending over the telescope all night he needed to stretch his legs. The sun's golden rays lit the pine trees, then the valley far below. Later he would develop and study the photos, but first he needed to get some sleep.

He did not mind the cold and sleepless nights. He was on a quest to find the answers to the mysteries of our universe.

Hubble had studied for many years to become an astronomer. Using his observations and measurements of the night sky, he tried to come up with theories to explain how our universe worked. Hubble never lost interest in solving these puzzles. The fun for him was not just in knowing what was true, but in figuring out the answers. When a reporter asked him what lies behind scientists' interest in astronomy, he replied, "Sheer curiosity. It's the basis of all science."[2]

Edwin Hubble devoted his life to studying the night sky. Slowly he began to find the answers for which he was searching. One of his greatest discoveries was that there are billions of galaxies beyond our Milky Way. He proved that the Milky Way was not the only galaxy out in space as once thought. Then he devised a way to classify galaxies.

He also confirmed that all these galaxies are speeding away from the earth. This proved that the universe was expanding. But why should the galaxies be racing apart? Why should the universe be expanding? Together with other astronomers he helped to find the answers to these questions. His scientific research changed our understanding of the universe forever.[3]

1

School Days

SHORTLY BEFORE EDWIN'S EIGHTH
birthday, his grandfather, Dr. William James, put
together a telescope. Edwin asked his grandfather if
he could stay up late to look through the telescope.
It would be a special treat.[1]

The night of Edwin's eighth birthday, Dr. James
took Edwin out to the dark hills behind the village
of Marshfield, Missouri. Away from the glow of
streetlights, thousands of stars sparkled in the sky.
Through the telescope, millions of stars shone bright
as diamonds. His grandfather told him that the stars
were really great suns. These suns were trillions of
miles away from the earth. Perhaps it was this event
that first sparked Edwin's interest in astronomy.

Life at the Hubble Household

Edwin was born on November 20, 1889, at his
grandparents' house in Marshfield. Edwin was the

third of seven children. Henry and Lucy were older than Edwin. Next came William, Helen, Emma Jane, and Elizabeth, who ranged down to fifteen years younger than he.[2]

John Powell Hubble was a stern father. He ordered dinner to be served at six-thirty every evening. After dinner the children all worked quietly on their homework. Edwin's father and mother, Virginia Lee James, known as "Jennie," encouraged their children to get a good education. His father, an insurance agent, hoped that his son would become a lawyer.

Edwin earned good grades in elementary school except for spelling. He liked to read, but was not a bookworm. He wandered through the woods observing the birds and animals, swimming in streams, or searching for arrowheads in the open fields. This love of the outdoors remained with him throughout his life. As an adult, he especially enjoyed nature through his favorite sport, trout fishing.

He and his friend Sam Shelton talked their parents into allowing them to observe a total lunar eclipse. They saw the eclipse begin at midnight and watched in awe as the Earth's shadow crept like a rusty smudge over the moon, then moved slowly away until the moon shone brightly again.[3]

When Edwin was twelve, the family moved to Wheaton, Illinois. At first, the Hubbles lived in a big Victorian house on Franklin Street. Here, Edwin and his brothers and sisters had plenty of room to play. There were eight bedrooms on the second floor as well as an attic, a tower, and a big basement.

Edwin entered Central School in Wheaton, starting in the eighth grade. At this school, known as the "Old Red Castle," he did well academically. He scored between 90 and 100 in most subjects.[4] Though his teachers said he was bright, some thought him a smart aleck. It seemed that Edwin, who was always the youngest in his class by two years, sometimes liked to show off. Even as an adult he enjoyed being the center of attention.[5]

In his junior year at high school he reached his full height of six feet two inches.[6] Edwin was active in athletics. He played well on the school basketball and football teams. On the track team he set records in the pole vault, shot put, standing high jump, running high jump, discus, and hammer throw.

When Edwin was twelve, his family moved into a large house in Wheaton, Illinois, where he would live until leaving for college. Pictured are Edwin, his sister, Lucy, brother William, and a cousin (far left).

Shooting for the Stars

It seems that Edwin liked challenges. In high school he learned about the Rhodes Scholarships. Students awarded a Rhodes Scholarship spent three years studying at the famous university in Oxford, England. The scholarship would pay for all their expenses. The scholars also received $1,500. Edwin began planning ahead to compete for one. His first step was to win a scholarship to college. He kept up his grades. He took Latin and German, history, chemistry, English, geography, algebra, and geometry. He graduated from high school, earning As in every subject.

On graduation night, Superintendent Russell presented the awards. Before he declared the winner of the scholarship to the University of Chicago, he said, "Edwin Hubble, I have watched you for four years and I have never seen you study for ten minutes."[7] Then with a mischievious smile on his face he announced Edwin the winner. The first challenge Edwin had set for himself was behind him; now he was off to college.

A photograph from a camping trip taken in southern Indiana some time around 1914. Edwin Hubble sits in back, between two other young men.

2

College Years

AT SIXTEEN, EDWIN BECAME A FRESHMAN at the University of Chicago. The university's gray stone buildings, though new, looked old. The pointed arches and high towers looked like those of the famous old university of Oxford, England, where Edwin still planned to go. While at the University of Chicago Edwin continued to work toward winning a Rhodes Scholarship. With this scholarship he would study at Oxford, after graduating from Chicago.

His father decided that he should live away from home, so Edwin joined a fraternity, Kappa Sigma.[1] This fraternity chose star athletes for its members. Since Edwin had done well in football, track, and basketball in high school, they gladly accepted him.

His father also had decided that Edwin should prepare for law school. Edwin really wanted to be an astronomer, but his father would never approve. He did not dare argue with his father, but he secretly planned a career in astronomy.[2]

Aiming to Please

He started taking the scientific subjects that he needed for astronomy. He took algebra, geometry, trigonometry, chemistry, surveying, and descriptive astronomy. To please his father he also took subjects that he needed to get into law school.

Though two years younger than most of his classmates, he excelled in school and in athletics. Although he put a lot into his studies, Edwin took time out for sports and other activities. He played on the basketball team, and was a member of the track team. In both sports he earned letters. Edwin also took up boxing. Although he wanted to play on the college football team, his parents would not allow it.[3]

In his second year Edwin continued to study mathematics and physics. Edwin was lucky to have the best professors teaching him. Professor Albert A. Michelson had just won the Nobel Prize for his work in measuring the speed of light. Professor Robert Millikan would also become a Nobel Prize winner. Edwin wanted to get a job as Millikan's laboratory assistant, so he studied hard.[4]

17

Edwin Hubble (top row, center) with his friends at the University of Chicago.

In his third year at college Edwin did so well that he won a Junior College Scholarship in Physics. He also got the job that he wanted in Millikan's laboratory.

A Dream Fulfilled

Edwin kept on working toward winning a Rhodes Scholarship. He took science courses and French, Latin, and Greek. He knew that Rhodes Scholars had to be well rounded. They had to participate in other activities. He joined a group called the Blackfriars. They put on musical comedies. Edwin, who had a good voice, sang in the group's choir.

During the summers, Edwin worked for the railroad. He worked in the woods around the Great Lakes, mapping land along the railroad's tracks. Years later Edwin liked to tell tall tales of his adventures in the wild.

In his fourth and final year at college Edwin, with his eyes on the Rhodes Scholarship, studied Latin. In a letter to his grandfather he said, "Study has been my middle name."[5]

He had to take a difficult exam to qualify for the scholarship. To prove that he could be a leader, he ran for vice president of his class and won.

In addition to being an excellent student, Hubble also played on the University of Chicago basketball team. Hubble is in the middle row, second from the left.

Edwin passed the scholarship exam with excellent scores. Five other students competing with him did not. Professor Millikan wrote a letter to the selection committee that said Edwin was "a man of magnificent physique, admirable scholarship, and worthy and lovable character."[6] Next Edwin had to go for an interview. Although we do not know what took place at the interview it must have gone well.

His years of preparation for the scholarship paid off. Hubble was voted the 1910 Rhodes Scholar from Illinois. His dream had come true. Now he would be going to England for three years.

Queen's College, Oxford

BEFORE LEAVING FOR ENGLAND, EDWIN spent the summer of 1910 with his family. The family had moved from Wheaton, Illinois, to Shelbyville, Kentucky, where John Hubble worked as an insurance agent. John was not well. He had malaria, a common disease at that time.

On Sundays the Hubbles opened their home to friends. Edwin's mother Jennie made sure that there was lemonade, tea, and freshly baked treats. His older sister Lucy played the piano. His younger brother Bill played the mandolin, and John played the violin. Edwin did not play an instrument, but sang along with them.

That year Halley's comet could be seen in the night sky. The comet, named for the British astronomer Edmund Halley, is very bright when it returns to the inner solar system, which it does every seventy-six years. In 1910, Earth would pass very close to the comet, even passing through the comet's tail. This worried many people.

During the week of the closest approach to the comet, the Hubbles gathered outside to gaze at it. They waited for darkness to fall and watched for the long, luminous tail of the comet to appear, seemingly hanging like a fine, thin veil in the night sky.

The summer passed quickly, and soon it was time to say goodbye. On September 7, Edwin traveled by train to Montreal, Canada. Together with eleven fellow Rhodes Scholars he boarded the ship *Canada* for an eleven-day voyage across the Atlantic Ocean bound for England. If he could have seen into the future, he would have known that this would be the first of many ocean crossings.

Going British

Oxford University was made up of twenty different colleges. Edwin had chosen Queen's College. He liked Queen's with its beautiful old buildings and gardens.

At Queen's he could study subjects required for both law and astronomy. His grandfather and his father wanted him to become a lawyer. To continue

When Hubble was sent to study at Oxford University as a Rhodes Scholar, he began acting as if he were an English gentleman. Pipe smoking is a habit he picked up during his stay.

to please them, Edwin studied law.[1] He also took courses related to astronomy.

He made friends with the American students at Oxford. Edwin admired the British way of life, so he also wanted to make British friends to get to know more about their customs. He started to speak with a British accent. He even wore English clothing. He took to wearing wool jackets, knickers, and a black cape, and even carried a cane—all in fashion at Oxford. He also took up pipe smoking. His American friends and some of his professors laughed at his fake British accent and manners. Yet from that time on Edwin kept to these ways.[2]

Though Edwin studied law (jurisprudence), he did not lose interest in astronomy. It was not easy to study law and astronomy at the same time, but Edwin found a way to do it. His friends asked why he studied law if he was more interested in astronomy. He told them that he would have to make money when he returned home. He did not tell them that his father would not accept astronomy as a useful career for his son.[3]

To keep fit Edwin took up "tubbing," or rowing. He learned how to row a scull, a racing boat with two men and two oars. He captained the baseball team. In track he won first place in the high jump.

Discovering the "Great End"

Most afternoons and evenings he spent studying in his room. At times he became discouraged. In a letter to his mother he said that unless work was toward some "great end," he did not find it very satisfying. He wrote, "I sometimes feel that there is within me, to do what the average man would not do, if only I find some principle, for whose sake I would leave everything else and devote my life."[4] He did not say what his "great end" or goal was. We can only guess that he was unhappy at having to study law, when he really wanted to be an astronomer.

Edwin visited Herbert Hall Turner, Oxford's professor of astronomy and director of the University Observatory. Edwin and Professor Turner took walks round the tower observatory. We do not know what they talked about, perhaps the unsolved puzzles of the universe. He spent some free weekends at the grand country homes of his new English friends. During Christmas, Easter, and summer vacations he took trips to explore Europe.

Back home, however, things were not going well. His father had malaria and a fatal liver disease. Edwin was not told that his father was so seriously ill. John Hubble died soon after, surrounded by his family. Only Edwin was not present.

Edwin stayed at Oxford that spring. He successfully completed his jurisprudence course and also studied Spanish. At the end of three years Edwin stated that he would practice law when he returned to the United States.[5] He wrote to his mother, telling her that he would do whatever he could to help his family. Though Edwin had good intentions, his career would soon take him far away from them. Astronomy would become the most important part of his life.

The Yerkes Observatory

HUBBLE RETURNED TO HIS FAMILY IN Louisville, Kentucky, after his father's death in 1913. With John gone, the eight members of the Hubble family had to work hard to put food on the table. It was not easy for him to settle back into everyday work. He missed England. On Sundays he had his mother prepare a special English tea for his Rhodes Scholar friends. With his Louisville friends, he took long hikes into the country. He told them stories about his days in Oxford and his cycling trips through Europe.

Soon after returning home, Hubble took the Kentucky bar examination. Today, in order to pass the bar, lawyers must pass a difficult examination. In 1913 there was no written examination. Instead, Hubble would have visited a neighboring circuit court judge with a gift, usually Kentucky bourbon or a box of cigars. The judge would have quizzed him on his knowledge of the law. Afterward he would have instructed him on the duties of a lawyer.[1] Though Hubble later said that his father's friends gave him legal work for which he earned a high salary, he never practiced law in Kentucky.[2] We can only guess why Hubble would have fibbed about this. Instead he took a job at New Albany High School in Indiana.[3]

There he taught Spanish, physics, and mathematics. He also coached basketball. He coached the team to an undefeated season, its best ever. The students admired the tall handsome Hubble, with his British accent and British ways. To them, he seemed to be a gentleman of the world.[4]

At the end of the school year in 1914, Hubble wrote to Forest Ray Moulton, his astronomy professor at the University of Chicago. He told the professor that he wanted to enter graduate school, but he needed financial help. Moulton told Hubble to apply for a job with Edwin B. Frost, director of the University of Chicago's Yerkes Observatory. Hubble said that he "chucked the law for astronomy, and I knew that even if I were second-rate or third-rate, it was astronomy that mattered."[5]

Frost jumped at the chance to have Hubble work as his assistant. He had an excellent education, and he had laboratory experience. During his summer jobs with the railroad he had learned surveying. Moulton wrote a letter to Frost full of praise for Hubble. With all this in his favor, Frost gave Hubble enough scholarship money to start postgraduate work leading to a doctoral degree in astronomy. Hubble would also serve as Frost's observatory assistant. At long last Hubble had begun his career as an astronomer.

A Bright New Career

The Yerkes Observatory was built away from the city lights of Chicago. It stood on the shores of Wisconsin's Lake Geneva, near the village of Williams Bay. It opened in 1897, seventeen years before Hubble came to work there. At the time it housed the world's largest refracting telescope. It is still the largest refracting telescope in the world. This telescope gathers light by means of a lens.

The 40-inch refractor lens, with a steel tube 60 feet long, looked like a giant gun pointing to the sky. It weighed six tons. High above, a huge dome covered the telescope like an upside-down bowl. At the press of a button, the floor rose to carry the astronomer to the level of the telescope. When the floor moved, it shook and creaked like the deck of a ship plowing through the waves.

When Hubble arrived at the observatory in August 1914, he discovered that Frost was going blind. Hubble had to read aloud to him. Worse yet, Frost could no longer see through the telescope.

The Yerkes Observatory staff poses for a picture beside the 60-inch refracting telescope. Hubble is in the back row, second from the right.

Frost's other assistants had already gone out West, where the new scientific advances were being made. Though he could not foresee it, Hubble would be joining them in a few years. There he would work with the even more powerful Mount Wilson telescope.

Over the next two years Hubble did not take many courses in astronomy because few were offered. He spent most of his time observing the night skies through the 24-inch reflector built by George Ritchey. With the Ritchey telescope and camera he took photographs of nebulae.

Studying Nebulae

At that time, many astronomers thought that all nebulae were clouds of dust and gas. These nebulae could be seen as faint circles and swirls of light. No one knew exactly what they were, but those who thought they were dust and gas concluded that they must be parts of the Milky Way, along with our sun and all the other stars in the sky. Perhaps each spiral nebula was a cloud from which a new star was forming. On the other hand, some other astronomers thought that the spiral nebulae were great galaxies like our own Milky Way, but far away from us. If this were true, then each spiral nebula was a galaxy, and each galaxy, or "island universe," would contain many billions of stars.

Then in 1913 the astronomer Vesto Melvin Slipher announced the surprising discovery that some spiral nebulae were hurtling away from us at great speeds. Slipher announced this finding at a meeting of the American Astronomical Society. Because anything moving away so fast could not be part of our Milky Way, Slipher's discovery seemed to support the theory that the spiral nebulae were really distant galaxies. Still, no one could prove that the nebulae were vast clouds of stars. Astronomers debated the nature of spiral nebulae for another ten years, until Hubble, using more powerful telescopes than were available in 1913, proved that they were, indeed, other galaxies in the universe.

Hubble, a twenty-four-year-old student, sat in the audience when Slipher announced his discovery. He must have puzzled over its meaning. He decided to study spiral nebulae while at the Yerkes Observatory. He trained the 24-inch reflector on a nebula and began photographing it.[6] He made hundreds of glass-plate photographs

Edwin Hubble stands in the top row, third from the left, in this 1916 staff picture at Yerkes Observatory.

of nebulae not seen before. Then he compared his plates with those taken by other astronomers. He confirmed that most were found in clusters outside the plane of the Milky Way. Could they be galaxies outside our own? Until astronomers could figure out their distance with the aid of more powerful telescopes, no one could be certain.

Hubble's work impressed Professor Frost. He showed Hubble's photographs of the spiral nebulae to other scientists at the meeting of the National Academy of Science. In his second year Hubble was awarded a grant. He used the money to continue his studies. In May 1916 he returned to the University of Chicago to complete his Ph.D. in astronomy. He took courses in celestial mechanics and mathematics.

For Hubble things were going very well. For his family these were difficult times.

Abandoning the Past

Edwin's father had died, and his mother and sisters moved to Madison, Wisconsin, where they rented a small house. Edwin occasionally came from Chicago and Yerkes to visit them. Henry, like his father before him, worked in the insurance business. Helen began classes at the University of Wisconsin. Lucy taught piano. Bill, the youngest brother, helped his family the most. Bill supported his mother for the rest of her life. Hubble never sent any money to her. We do not know why. Perhaps, like a mountain climber, he focused his mind and energy on reaching his goal. He never looked back.

5

Off to War!

IN NOVEMBER 1916, HUBBLE RECEIVED
an important letter. It came from Dr. George
Ellery Hale, director of Mount Wilson Observatory
in California. Like Hubble, Hale was searching for
answers to the riddles of the universe. Hale
offered Hubble a job as an astronomer at Mount
Wilson.

A giant telescope, the 100-inch Hooker, was
being built on Mount Wilson. It would be the most
powerful reflecting telescope in the world. Without
Hale's hard work and vision it would not have
been built. Back in 1890 Hale began to dream of
giant reflecting telescopes that would look into the
depths of space.

Hale had already built the 40-inch refractor at
the Yerkes Observatory in Wisconsin. But it was not
big enough. He moved to California and built the
60-inch reflector on Mount Wilson. By 1916 he

was building the 100-inch telescope on Mount Wilson. Thirty years later Hale would come up with an even more daring plan. He would build a telescope with a diameter twice as large, and ten times as costly.[1]

Hubble could not have wished for a better chance to advance his career. However, because of World War I he did not take the job right away. He decided to join the Army instead. Then he sent a telegram to Hale: "Regret cannot accept your invitation to join the Mount Wilson staff. Joined the Army instead. Am off to war."[2] Hale promised to hold his position at Mount Wilson until he returned from the Army.

World War I had started in Europe in 1914. Millions of young men died in muddy trenches, and on bloody battlefields. Women and children starved. Hubble considered it his duty to help defend England.[3]

A Rush to Finish

Because Hubble had to report to the Army, he rushed to complete the writing of his dissertation for the doctorate degree. Yet he thought out the right questions to ask. He had the courage and self-confidence to question the picture of the universe then accepted by most scientists.[4]

The title of the dissertation was "Photographic Investigations of Faint Nebulae." To prepare for his dissertation, Hubble had spent many long hours photographing nebulae. He had made over a thousand photographs, each needing an exposure of at least two hours. This part of Hubble's work took a lot of patience; it could not be hurried. From the plates he sorted 511 nebulae into groups. He sorted the nebulae by size, brightness, and shape. He also showed that most of these nebulae could be seen in clusters in directions other than the plane of the Milky Way. Though Hubble's thesis was "not very good technically. . . . It shows clearly the hand of a great scientist groping toward the solution of great problems."[5]

Hubble would need to do much more research before he could be certain about the nebulae. He wondered if they were separate galaxies. Exactly how could they be classified? In the years to come, his work with Mount Wilson's 100-inch telescope, as well as improvements in photography and spectroscopy, and new physical and mathematical theories, would help him find the answers to these

In 1916, a 100-inch telescope was built on Mount Wilson. Hubble would use this telescope to make some of his most famous discoveries.

very complex questions. Right then, however, he was off to fight a war.

Reporting for Duty

Hubble reported for duty at Fort Sheridan on Lake Michigan. Hubble, always athletic, excelled at the hard physical training. He was put in charge of training the other men. A month later he became Captain Hubble. A year later he earned the rank of major.

Major Edwin Hubble with his sister, Lucy, a Red Cross
nurse, during World War I. In 1917, Hubble joined the
United States Army because he felt it was his duty to
help defend England.

Hubble looked forward to being shipped overseas. It was fourteen months before he sailed out from New York Harbor on the *Walmar Castle*. He did his best to stay on submarine patrol, even though he felt seasick. After ten days of stormy seas his ship arrived in Glasgow, Scotland.[6]

From Glasgow his infantry division, the Black Hawks, went to Southampton, England. From Southampton the men were ferried across the English Channel to LeHavre, France. Hubble hoped that he would at last get into active combat against the Germans. It was too late, however, for the war was drawing to a close. Hubble wrote to a friend, "I barely got under fire and altogether I am disappointed in the matter of the war."[7] Though he could not know it, he would get the chance to serve in another world war.

Hubble had survived tough training and had crossed dangerous waters filled with enemy submarines. He even lived through the great flu epidemic. His training in the Army influenced his behavior. In later years he liked to be called "Major," and he liked to run things with strict military discipline.

6

Mount Wilson

WITH THE WAR OVER, HUBBLE TRAVELED to Pasadena, California, to start work at the Mount Wilson Observatory. In 1919 Pasadena was still a small town surrounded by open country, orange groves, and vineyards. He rented rooms in a house near the observatory offices.[1] When not working at the office studying photographs, Hubble worked at the observatory.

The astronomers competed for time on the telescope. Hubble had to wait six weeks after his arrival before getting his turn on the mountain. His first observatory run came on the 10-inch Cooke telescope, and then the 60- inch telescope. On Christmas Eve he worked on the 100-inch.

Life on the Mountain
Hubble was always ready for work on the mountain. After breakfast he would pull out his

war-time suitcase labeled, "Major Edwin P. Hubble, 343rd Inf." In it he packed clothing, books, a tin of tobacco, and a flashlight. An observatory truck took him from Santa Barbara Street up the narrow winding Mount Wilson Toll Road. It zigzagged up the San Gabriel Mountains to the observatory on the peak. The Toll Road was first used to carry up parts of the observatory's solar towers as well as the 60-inch and 100-inch telescopes.

At the top of Mount Wilson, Hubble had a breathtaking view. To the west and south he could see central Los Angeles. On a clear day he could even see the Pacific Ocean and offshore islands. To the southwest he could see Mount Harvard with the Mount Wilson Toll Road snaking along the edge. He walked over to the living quarters to unpack his things. The living quarters were called the Monastery because women were banned from them. Only the cook and housekeeper could go inside.

His most important work on the mountain began after dinner. Then he would enter the observatory, climb the stairs to the observing platform, and take his place at the great telescope. He worked through the night until dawn's first light dimmed the sky.[2]

Hale's Dream

At Mount Wilson, Hubble worked with some of the best astronomers in the world. George Hale, Mount Wilson's first director, had first dreamed of an observatory atop the mountain in 1903. He persuaded the scientists at the Carnegie Institution of Washington to give $150,000 to help build it. Then he sold John D. Hooker, a Los Angeles businessman, on his dream. Hooker gave money to purchase a 100-inch diameter mirror for the telescope.

However, Hale's dream almost turned into a nightmare. No factory had made a glass disc that would be used to make the mirror, as large as the one needed for Mount Wilson. The St. Gobain glassworks in Paris agreed to make it. They used green glass normally used for making wine bottles. After much trial and error, St. Gobain made a giant disk. The disk, 101 inches across and 13 inches thick, weighed over five tons. It was shipped across the Atlantic to New York, then to New Orleans before reaching Santa Barbara, California.

When it finally arrived at the optical shop in Santa Barbara, the technician in charge unpacked and examined it. To Hale's dismay he found air

A bird's-eye perspective of the Mount Wilson Observatory.

bubbles and weak spots in the glass. He refused to polish the disk. St. Gobain then agreed to make a second disk without charge. After months of work it cracked while cooling in horse manure. Hale refused to give up.

Two years later, in 1910, an expert from the Corning Glass Company in the United States reexamined the first glass disk. After testing, he found that the bubbles strengthened rather than weakened the glass. Then he convinced the opticians to begin grinding down the glass.

The shape of the mirror had to be perfect to within a few millionths of an inch. The technicians worked in a special room to make sure that nothing scuffed the glass. They used distilled water and jeweler's powder to polish the glass perfectly smooth. To stop any dust from touching the glass, the room had sealed windows and doors. Air in the room was filtered clean. The workers wore surgical gowns and caps. The walls were painted glossy white. The floors were kept wet to prevent dust from getting onto the glass. It took five years to complete grinding and smoothly polishing the 7,800 square inches of glass. They removed one ton of glass from the surface to give it a particular shape (called a paraboloid), which could focus light from a distant star to a single point.

Then they poured chemicals over the glass to deposit a very thin layer of silver on the polished surface. When the chemicals were drained off, the glass disk had become a perfectly shaped and silvered mirror. The total amount of silver in the thin layer that remained on the glass amounted to no more than a silver 25-cent coin. The giant mirror would now make visible billions more stars than any previous telescopes.[3]

While the opticians worked on the glass, Hale had a domed observatory built on the mountain. Workers poured concrete and steel into the observatory floor to support the telescope. A steel frame was erected for mounting the telescope. The frame rested on ball bearings so that the telescope could be moved easily. The whole structure could be moved by hand because the ball bearings floated in a tank of mercury.

When the observatory was nearly complete, the 100-inch mirror had to be moved up the mountain. A truck, with four motors to turn each wheel, transported it and building materials up the mountain. A team of mules pulled the truck up the steepest part of the road.[4]

It had taken eleven years for Hale's dream to come true. With this telescope, Hubble could measure the distance of galaxies. Today the telescope is rated as a mechanical masterpiece. It is an International Historical Mechanical Engineering Landmark.

The Great Debate

HUBBLE WAS FOLLOWING IN THE footsteps of famous astronomers: Copernicus, Kepler, Galileo, Newton, and Herschel. They were his heroes.[1] One day *he* might be the one to find answers to the unsolved puzzles. He spoke of his research as an "adventure." He said, "The romance of science lies in its explorations. Equipped with his five senses man explores the universe around him and calls the adventure Science."[2]

Almost four hundred years ago Galileo had looked through a telescope and discovered that the Milky Way was made up of millions of stars. From that time on astronomers have asked: Is the Milky Way our entire universe? Are there countless systems of suns so distant from us that we cannot see them? Some astronomers thought that there were many other galaxies or "island universes." Others thought there was just one (our own). Only

47

with more powerful telescopes could this question be answered beyond a doubt.

Herschel's Influence

The German-English astronomer William Herschel, who lived from 1738–1822, tried to find the answer. Herschel built the largest and most accurate reflecting telescope in the world at that time.

For thirty years Herschel and his sister Caroline observed the heavens and discovered hundreds of new stars and thousands of nebulae. However, his telescope was not powerful enough to see if the nebulae were gas clouds or gigantic collections of stars. Nor could Herschel measure how far away they were. He concluded that the nebulae were part of the Milky Way.

For nearly a hundred and fifty years after Herschel, astronomers thought that the Milky Way galaxy was all there was in the universe. A Dutch astronomer, Jacobus Cornelis Kapteyn, who lived from 1851–1922, continued Herschel's work. From 1908–1913, Kapteyn came to work at the Mount Wilson Observatory for a few months each year. Kapteyn, like Herschel, had concluded that all the stars we see are part of the same galaxy, but some look dimmer because they are farther away.

Later, astronomers improved on Herschel's methods. They had better telescopes and they used photography to take pictures of the sky. On a photograph they could carefully count the stars. Harlow Shapley (1885–1972) became famous for showing that the sun was not at the center of the galaxy as Herschel had thought, but was to one side. Yet Shapley, using measurements made by the astronomer Adriaan van Maanen, thought that there was only one galaxy. (Later, Hubble showed that van Maanen had made wrong measurements.)

Hubble's Rivals

Van Maanen had already spent years taking photographs of spiral nebulae before Hubble started working at Mount Wilson. He resented having to share the 100-inch telescope with Hubble, which was one reason they did not seem to get along.[3]

Shapley did not like Hubble either. Shapley thought that Hubble was a snob. They were both from Missouri, but Hubble never spoke about his roots in Missouri. He liked to speak with a British accent, and dressed as if he were an English

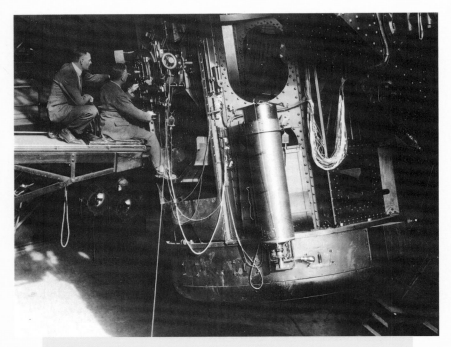

Edwin Hubble and Sir James Hopwood Jeans at the 100-inch Hooker telescope, around 1931.

gentleman. The men became open rivals a few years later when Hubble found evidence to challenge Shapley and van Maanen.

Other astronomers besides Hubble thought that van Maanen and Shapley were mistaken. Deep in the southern sky, astronomers could see two foggy patches of light. The patches looked as though they had broken loose from the Milky Way. They are named the Magellanic Clouds, after the

Portuguese navigator Ferdinand Magellan. Were the Magellanic Clouds part of the Milky Way or separate from it? To find the answer to this question the astronomers needed to know how far away they were from the Milky Way. If the Magellanic Clouds were very distant from the Milky Way they could not be part of it. But how distant were they?

Cepheids and Novae

Henrietta Swan Leavitt, who lived from 1868–1921, was an American astronomer who discovered one way to measure stellar distances. In 1912 Leavitt was studying variable stars called Cepheids. Cepheids are stars that grow brighter and dimmer *over a set time or period*. Each Cepheid cycles from brighter to dimmer and back over a fixed period of time. Some take only a few days; others take months. Leavitt noticed that the greater the brightness of the Cepheid, the longer its period—the time it takes to go from bright to dim. This made it possible, using mathematic calculations, to work out the distances between objects in the galaxy.

Suppose an astronomer sees two Cepheids, each with the same period. That would mean that the two Cepheids would be equally bright when viewed from the same distance. Suppose, however, one of those Cepheids appears to be much brighter than the other. Then that can only be because the brighter Cepheid is closer than the dimmer one. If you see two street lights shining in the distance, you reason that the brighter one is closer to you than the dimmer one because they actually have equal luminosities.

Using Henrietta Leavitt's Cepheids, astronomers were able to work out a rough distance to the Magellanic Clouds. In the universe, distance is measured by the speed of light, which is 186,000 miles per second. A "light-year" is the distance that light travels in a year, which is a long way because of the great speed of light. (One light-year is about 6 trillion miles!) By about 1920, astronomers were pretty sure that the Magellanic Clouds were some 80,000 light-years or more away. (Modern measurements place the Large Magellanic Cloud at about 180,000 light-years and the Small Magellanic Cloud at around 200,000 light-years distance.) At the time, these were the most distant known objects in the universe, which led many astronomers to wonder if our whole universe were made up of only our Milky Way galaxy along with the smaller satellite galaxies, the Magellanic Clouds.

There was another piece of the puzzle still unsolved. In 1612 German astronomer Simon Marius, who lived from 1570–1624, noticed a dim patch of light in the constellation Andromeda. Because it looked like a cloud, or nebula, astronomers at first thought that it was made of swirling dust and gas.

Then astronomers noticed that from time to time tiny points of light appeared in Andromeda. They thought that these lights might be novae. Novae are stars that suddenly brighten and then fade away. Astronomers wondered if these novae were *inside* the Andromeda nebula or *in front* of the nebula.

Heber D. Curtis, who lived from 1872–1942, studied this problem. He noticed that many novae appeared in the Andromeda nebula, but very few appeared elsewhere in the sky. Why should so many novae appear only in the space in front of Andromeda? Shouldn't they then appear in other parts of space? It did not make sense that the space in front of the Andromeda nebula was completely different from any other space in the sky.

Curtis also noticed that the novae in Andromeda were very dim. They were dimmer than the novae he saw in other parts of the sky. Could it be that the Andromeda nebula was formed by stars beyond our galaxy? For years astronomers could not prove Curtis's ideas.

Shapely vs. Curtis

Astronomers continued to debate. Some astronomers thought that the universe was a single big galaxy (Shapley and van Maanen). Others thought that the nebulae were external galaxies (Curtis and Hubble).[4] In 1920 at the National Academy of Science in Washington, D.C., Shapley and Curtis took opposite sides of what came to be called "The Great Debate."

Shapley argued that the Milky Way was the only galaxy in the universe. He asserted that spiral nebulae were nebulous objects inside our galaxy. Curtis challenged his view. He thought that there were many other galaxies in space. He argued that the Andromeda nebula lay outside our own stellar system, and that the spirals were island universes like our own galaxy. At the time both Shapley and

Curtis thought that *they* had won the debate. Hubble read and studied the Shapley–Curtis debate very carefully.

Just three years later, using the power of the new Mount Wilson 100-inch telescope, he would settle the debate. He would prove that Curtis's argument was correct. Our Milky Way is only one of thousands of galaxies in a universe stretching for tens of millions of light-years. This breakthrough would make Hubble a famous astronomer.

In the Depths of Space

IN THE SUMMER OF 1923 HUBBLE carefully observed the Andromeda nebula with the 60- and 100-inch reflectors. Even on nights when the sky clouded over he patiently took photographs.[1] He obtained his first good plates of the Andromeda galaxy (M31) on October 5–6 with the 100-inch.[2] The plate numbered H335H became the most famous ever taken. It changed our view of the universe forever.

A Brilliant Discovery

Hubble found three novae. He marked these with an *N* for *nova*. When he looked more closely he saw that one was a faint Cepheid variable star. Hubble crossed out the letter *N* and put in large letters "VAR!" *VAR* stood for *variable*.

Like a smart detective he looked at plates that the Mount Wilson astronomer George W. Ritchey had taken fifteen years before. He found the same variable star on Ritchey's plates. From these he figured the period—the time it took for the star to go from bright to dim and bright again—for the period-luminosity curve of Henrietta Leavitt. Still, Hubble wanted even more exact measurements. To get them he photographed the Andromeda nebula for nearly a week. No one had tried to find Cepheids in the Andromeda nebula before.

With these new plates he could see clearly that the star was a Cepheid going into its brightest stage. From its period and apparent brightness, the distance of the Andromeda galaxy could be calculated. Using Henrietta Leavitt's period-luminosity curve, Hubble figured the luminosity of the star. He knew that two Cepheids having the same period would have the same luminosity and therefore would appear equally bright when viewed from the same distance. One of the Cepheids, however, may appear to be much brighter than the other because the brighter Cepheid is closer than the dimmer one.

Then, using Shapley's tables of apparent and absolute magnitude, based on Leavitt's work, Hubble compared their brightness to estimate the

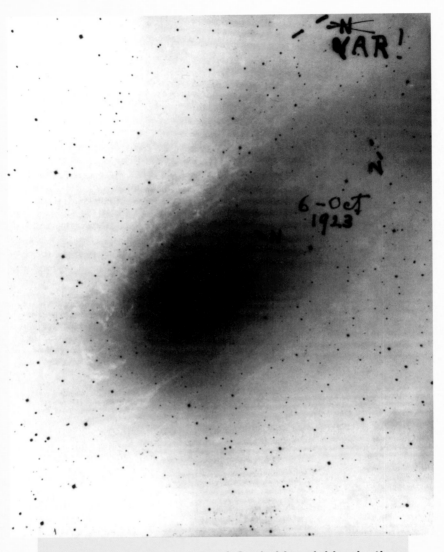

Hubble's discovery plate of Cepheid variables in the Andromeda Galaxy from October 5–6, 1923. This photo would forever change the world's understanding of the universe.

star's distance from the earth. Again, think of two *equally* bright street lights shining in the distance. If one looks brighter than the other you can guess that the brighter one is closer to you than the dimmer one. Hubble found that the Andromeda nebula lay at a distance of about a million light-years from us. Later, more accurate observations showed it to be 2,300,000 light-years away. Now he could prove that the Andromeda nebula was far beyond our Milky Way galaxy! Hubble knew that he had found the answer for which astronomers had been searching. There are other galaxies beyond our own![3]

Ending "The Great Debate"

Hubble did not rush to tell the whole world about his great discovery. He was a careful scientist. He wrote a letter to Shapley to tell him of his discovery. When Shapley read his letter, he said, "Here is the letter that has destroyed my universe."[4] Still, Hubble wanted to ensure that his results were as accurate as he could make them.

Over the next few months he observed many other variable stars in the Andromeda nebula. He used them to calculate distances from the earth. He showed that spiral nebulae, shaped like giant

Images of the Eagle Nebula and spiral galaxy M51 (NGC5194), known as the whirlpool galaxy, taken by the Hubble Telescope in January 2005.

pinwheels, were actually huge systems of stars. They are spiral galaxies similar to our own Milky Way galaxy, but unimaginably distant. They were not clouds of gas. They were not within our galaxy. Shapley and van Maanen could no longer argue with Hubble. "The Great Debate" was over.

Hubble wrote about his discoveries in a scientific paper, "Cepheids in Spiral Nebulae." Dr. Henry Norris Russell, a well-known astronomer, read Hubble's paper at a meeting of American

Association for the Advancement of Science (AAAS). Russell praised Hubble. He said that his work was the product of a young man of great ability. It had expanded one-hundred-fold the known universe. It settled the question of the nature of the spirals, showing them to be giant clusters of stars comparable with our own galaxy. The following year, in 1924, Hubble was honored with a prize from the AAAS. Since then astronomers have found millions of galaxies. We know now that the Milky Way, the Andromeda nebula, the Magellanic Clouds, and about a dozen other smaller galaxies form a cluster of galaxies called the "local group." Beyond them are countless other galaxies.

Scientists urged Hubble to publish his great discovery immediately. Hubble, however, waited another year before publishing. He wanted to be sure that van Maanen would not prove him wrong.[5]

Discovering Another Love

Although Hubble was hard at work, he found time to court Grace Burke Leib, with whom he had fallen in love. She shared Hubble's love of the outdoors. She liked books and read aloud to

61

Edwin Hubble and his wife, Grace.

Hubble.[6] He entertained Grace and her family with stories about his past adventures. Hubble's family was two thousand miles away, and he chose not to talk about them. Grace's father was a rich banker. Hubble knew that Grace was used to luxuries that he could not afford. Still, Grace understood his great love of astronomy. She encouraged him in his career, becoming his greatest admirer. They were married on February 26, 1924.

Grace devoted herself to writing a biography of her husband, whom she idolized. She kept journals of important events in their lives. These journals were not always accurate. Grace chose to leave out those things that were not complimentary to her husband.[7]

9

Classification of Galaxies

HUBBLE'S SCIENTIFIC CONTRIBUTIONS did not end with proving that there were other galaxies or island universes. He studied the hundreds of plates he had taken to see if he could find a way of sorting the galaxies (or nebulae, as he called them).

Hubble had been thinking about this since his work at the Yerkes Observatory. He sent his early classification system to the International Astronomical Union (IAU) in 1922, but the group did not publish it. Though disappointed, he kept working on it.[1]

A year later Hubble sent typed notes and photographs to his friend Vesto Melvin Slipher. He asked Slipher to show them to a group of astronomers. The group was called the Commission on Nebulae and Star Clusters. Hubble waited to hear from Slipher for seven months. Finally he sent Slipher a note saying that Hale, the director of Mount Wilson, wanted to publish his classification system. With this reminder, Slipher sent Hubble's classification to the commission. A few more months passed and still Hubble heard nothing. Would the commission accept it?

Hubble's System

Hubble had come up with an excellent system. He knew that most galaxies rotated about a central nucleus, which he called regular types. Only 3 percent did not, and he named these irregulars. He sorted the regulars into two main shapes, spirals and ellipticals. He then divided the spirals into normal and barred. These shapes made up a series, which Hubble called a family.

Our Milky Way is a spiral galaxy. Stars spiral out from its center like a giant pinwheel. It is disk-shaped with a central bulge and spiral arms. Our solar system is in one of these arms, about two-thirds of the way from the center.

With the aid of powerful telescopes, astronomers saw that the Milky Way's center was made of many old stars. The outward curving spiral arms were made of fewer young stars,

An artist's rendering of the Milky Way galaxy, released by the University of Wisconsin.

clusters of stars, and clouds of gas and dust called nebulae.

Besides studying the shapes of galaxies, Hubble explored objects in them. He found many types of bright objects: novae, globular clusters, gaseous nebulae, super-giant blue stars, red long-period variables, Cepheids, and others.

Disappointment and Deceit

At last Hubble got the decision of the commission. He was very disappointed. The scientists said that his classification scheme was interesting, but they decided not to accept it.

Though Hubble wanted the official approval of the commission, he decided to publish his classification without its support. Then came another shock. Just as he was ready to publish, astronomer Knut Lundmark put out a classification similar to his. Hubble was very upset and sent an angry letter to Slipher, protesting that Lundmark had stolen his scheme.

In the end Hubble decided to go ahead and publish his classification system. It is still used by astronomers today. Hubble's classification brought order to the confusion about galaxy forms and helped astronomers with their research.

10

The Big Bang

HUBBLE KNEW THAT IT WAS IMPORTANT for him to understand the new scientific ideas of the day. To keep up with new ideas Hubble met regularly with scientists to discuss their theories. He invited astronomers, mathematicians, and physicists to his home. After enjoying the food and drink that Grace provided, they would debate scientific theories. Hubble followed the scientists as they chalked math on a blackboard that he put up on the living room wall. He listened carefully to what they said, but he did not always agree with them.

On his travels in Europe, Hubble made sure that he visited the top astronomers. In 1928 he visited the Dutch astronomer Willem de Sitter in the Netherlands. De Sitter encouraged Hubble to keep working on Vesto Slipher's measurements of the speed of objects moving in space (radial velocity).

Prisms and Spectrums

In the late 1800s, scientists began to study light from the stars with special instruments. They already knew that when sunlight passes through a triangle of glass, called a prism, its rays bend. Sunlight is a mixture of small lightwaves of different lengths. The longer waves bend less than the shorter wavelengths when they pass through a prism. Therefore, a band of light is produced with the wavelengths lined up from the longest to the shortest. This band is called a spectrum. The spectrum looks like a rainbow because the wavelengths have different colors. Red, with the longest, is at one end; then orange, yellow, green, blue, and violet. Violet has the shortest wavelength. Although the solar spectrum appears continuous to the eye, scientists found there are gaps where a bit of the spectrum is missing in sunlight. These missing wavelengths show up as dark lines in the spectrum.

Astronomers used this knowledge to learn more about stars. Starlight, like sunlight, can be broken into a spectrum with dark lines. Astronomers have learned to recognize the pattern of dark lines for different stars. These discoveries opened the door to new discoveries and a new picture of the universe.

In 1929 Hubble and Milton Humason made an important discovery built on Slipher's earlier discoveries. In 1912 Slipher had photographed the spectrum of the Andromeda galaxy, although at that time, astronomers did not know it was a galaxy. He saw dark lines on its spectrum, just like those of starlight or sunlight.[1]

Over the next few years Slipher studied the spectra of fifteen other galaxies. Photographing spectra was no easy task. The observation of a single object took many nights. By the end of 1914 Slipher had made spectra of nearly forty nebulae and star clusters. To his surprise, thirteen were moving away from us at great speed. Later, Hubble solved Slipher's puzzle by proving that these nebulae were really distant galaxies. At the time Slipher also tried to measure the speeds at which the galaxies were moving, but without success.

As Hubble recorded light from distant galaxies with the 100-inch telescope, he noticed something strange. Instead of matching up with known wavelengths, the light from these galaxies was slightly shifted toward the red end of the spectrum. Hubble also noticed that in general the farther away the galaxy, the larger the shift toward the red end. This could be explained by the Doppler effect.

As a car speeds toward you, its sound seems to increase in pitch. As it moves away the pitch seems to decrease. This is called the Doppler effect. Light waves act similarly to sound waves. In other words, light waves coming from a star speeding away from earth will be shifted toward the red end of the spectrum. If the object is moving toward us, the spectrum shifts to violet.

From this Hubble reasoned that the change in location of lines in the spectrum of galaxies was evidence that galaxies are moving away from us. If the light is moving away, then the wavelengths of light we receive are lengthened. The dark lines shift toward the red end of the spectrum, and this gives the name *redshift*. Hubble was also able to detect the speed of the galaxy from the amount of shift.

Hubble now had all the information he needed to solve this problem. His teammate Humason helped him to find the answer to this puzzle. Humason's plates gave Hubble the important data he needed to show the relationship between speed and distance. Far galaxies receded, or moved away, faster than close ones.

Milton Humason

Humason had quit school at age fourteen. He got a job driving pack mules carrying supplies up the steep trails to Mount Wilson. Later he worked as a night assistant. He said, "I decided that the only way to stay awake all night was to get interested in what was going on. So I did."[2] He did such excellent work that he was promoted to staff astronomer.

With the 100-inch at Mount Wilson, Humason could photograph the light from distant galaxies. Because the light was so dim, Humason had to expose the photographic plate for many hours. Night after night Humason locked the telescope on an object for many hours. Sometimes the mechanism jammed and he had to hold the plates in place with his shoulder.

After spending so many sleepless nights on Mount Wilson, Humason was ready to quit. However, Hubble was determined to continue his research. With the help of George Hale, they talked Humason into continuing his work. They even promised him a new and improved spectrograph and camera. Humason stayed and photographed forty-five new spectra.

Hubble's Law

Using Humason's photographs, Hubble showed that in general the greater the redshift the more distant the object from the earth. In addition, the farther a galaxy the more quickly it is moving from earth. He was the first to prove that there was a link between distance and speed, as scientists had guessed.

Hubble demonstrated that the speed at which a galaxy is moving away from us is proportional to its distance from us. The more distant a galaxy, the greater its speed. This is called Hubble's law.

There were still more questions to be answered: *Why* were the galaxies speeding away from us? Scientists now believe that the universe began with a gigantic explosion, today called the Big Bang theory. All matter in the universe was once concentrated into a tight mass, a very hot, thick "soup" of particles of energy. Then about 13.7 billion years ago a massive explosion took place. The explosion caused the universe to expand. The material from this explosion slowly formed into galaxies, planets, and stars. Our sun formed 4.6 billion years ago. Earth and the other planets of our solar system were formed from leftover material surrounding the sun.

Imagine the universe as a loaf of bread dough with raisins sprinkled in it. As the dough rises during baking, the raisins begin to move away from one another. If the Milky Way was a raisin in this loaf, the neighboring raisins would seem to be moving away in all directions. This is because the dough between the two raisins is expanding. A raisin twice as far away would seem to be moving away twice as fast, because there is twice as much dough in between. The farther away the raisins, the faster they would seem to move away. Hubble reasoned that the earth, the Milky Way galaxy, and other objects in space are not expanding. The space between them is expanding. Hubble's theory became known as Hubble's expansion.

Today astronomers have a very accurate knowledge of the expansion rate of the universe, which is called the "Hubble Constant." The Hubble Space Telescope and other space observatories have made this possible. Measurement of the Hubble Constant, which has been confirmed by independent methods, allows us to calculate how much time has passed since the Big Bang, which means we can figure out the age of the universe to be 13.7 billion years.

These colorful, cosmic fireworks are actually sheets of debris from a stellar explosion in a neighboring galaxy. This material will eventually be recycled into a whole new generation of stars. Our own Sun and planets were created in a similar fashion from an explosion in the Milky Way galaxy billions of years ago.

Astronomers recognized the importance of this law as soon as Hubble began publishing his findings. The greatest scientist of the time, Albert Einstein, praised Hubble's work.[3] In just five years, from 1924 to 1929, Hubble had achieved the following outstanding results:

First, he had demonstrated that nebulae outside the Milky Way are distant galaxies, thus proving the island structure of the universe. Second, he worked out a classification of these galaxies. Finally, he discovered the awesome expansion of the universe. Just five years later he and Humason confirmed the redshift law. Not since Copernicus and Galileo had there been such major changes in our understanding of the universe. The universe could no longer be thought of as static. The universe is in a constant state of change or expansion.

From then on Hubble was recognized everywhere for his great achievements. He was invited to lecture at renowned universities. Many honors and medals were awarded to him. Hubble's work pushed the frontiers of the universe beyond the limits of our imagination. He opened the way for modern astronomers to reach out beyond our own galaxy into the depths of space.

11

Fame and Fortune

ON A WINTER MORNING IN 1931, HUBBLE drove up the steep dirt road to Mount Wilson with the world's most famous scientist, Albert Einstein. Einstein had come to visit Caltech and Mount Wilson from Berlin, Germany. Wherever he went, crowds would gather around him to get autographs and to take pictures.

When the men arrived at the observatory they visited the 150-foot tower telescope used to study the sun. Einstein was especially interested in seeing for himself how this 100-inch telescope worked. Hubble gave Einstein a turn at the 100-inch telescope. As he climbed to the platform Einstein called out nervously, "The mountain is spinning!" Hubble called back, "The dome is revolving and carrying you with it."[1] They stayed up through the night to view the planets Jupiter and Mars, the asteroid Eros, Sirius the "Dog Star," and other galaxies.

Later that year the Mount Wilson Observatory group gave a banquet in Einstein's honor. In his speech Einstein praised the work of two California scientists, Edwin Hubble and Richard Tolman. Einstein said that he had changed his theory of general relativity to keep the universe static (motionless). He called this his "worst blunder." Einstein said that Hubble and Tolman's work had altered his view of the universe from static to active. He could not deny the data showing that the universe was expanding.

A Celebrity Scientist

Hubble became a celebrity when news came out that his work had caused the great Einstein to change his view. Newspaper headlines told the world how the work of two American scientists had proved that the universe was expanding, and had caused Einstein to correct his theory.

All the publicity shone a spotlight on the Mount Wilson observatory. So many visitors wanted to see the observatory that they had to reserve tickets in advance. Hubble even gave tours to visiting celebrities.

May 6 1921

In 1921, legendary physicist Albert Einstein visited the Yerkes Observatory (above). By 1931, the work done by Hubble and fellow astronomer Richard Tolman caused Einstein to change his general theory of relativity.

By 1935 visitors no longer needed to travel the narrow, zigzagging path to the top. The paved Angeles Crest Highway replaced the old narrow road. Today the observatory grounds are on land owned by the U.S. Forest Service and are open to the public.

Hubble, an excellent speaker and writer, was invited to lecture at universities in the United States and Great Britain. He was elected to important scientific positions and received many scientific awards. The rich and famous wanted to meet him. Like a movie star, Hubble had an exciting personality.[2]

In 1935 Hubble was invited to lecture at his college in Oxford, England. Just as he was about to begin lecturing, he received news that Oxford was going to award him the honorary degree of Doctor of Science. His wife Grace noticed how surprised and proud Hubble was.[3] He would be the first Rhodes Scholar ever to receive this great honor. At the awards ceremony they praised him saying:

> We salute a former Rhodes scholar, who in his youth consecrated [pledged] himself to astronomy. . . . Here is a man who has discovered worlds far removed from ours, and he defined the laws of motion—for the more distant they are the faster they seem to be running away from us.[4]

Neglecting Work and Family

Afterward the Hubbles toured France and Germany for two months. During this time,

Hubble's mother Virginia died. She was buried in the Hubble family plot in Springfield, Missouri. Hubble had neglected his family over the years. He never returned to visit them, not even for his mother's funeral.

The Hubbles returned to California four months later. Hubble's bosses noticed that he had taken an extra-long vacation from work. They were not pleased.[5] His bosses, while agreeing that he was a brilliant scientist, said that he was not a team player. In the future they would vote against his becoming the director of the new Mount Palomar Observatory near San Diego.

The Realm of the Nebulae

IN 1934 HUBBLE PUBLISHED ANOTHER important scientific paper, "The Distribution of Extra-Galactic Nebulae." After looking at thousands of plates he concluded that galaxies are scattered evenly throughout space. Before this astronomers did not know if there were more galaxies in one part of space than another.

Even with these important discoveries, astronomers wanted to see deeper into space. They tried to photograph more and more distant, fainter objects. Yet even the great 100-inch telescope had its limits.

Hale's "Big Eye"

George Hale, who had built the Yerkes and Mount Wilson telescopes, began to dream about an even more powerful one on Mount Palomar, in Southern California. A telescope that would let astronomers explore even farther into space. It would have a mirror 200 inches in diameter, making it the world's largest camera as well. Its mirror, called the "Big Eye," would have the power of a million human eyes. It would see a candle 10,000 miles away. Hubble explained that the Palomar reflecting telescope would be capable of photographing the lettering on a silver dollar from 450 miles away.

Slowly Hale's plan took shape. A team of experts decided to make the mirror of pyrex glass. It was too large to be one solid disk. Instead, it would be divided into segments like a honeycomb. First, melted glass for the mirror was poured into a special mold. The glass had to be cooled slowly over ten months. Then, in 1935, the 40,000-pound disk, in a case of steel, was put onto a railroad car for its journey from New York to Pasadena, California. Here, workers waited to grind and polish it. Because of World War II, however, it took more than ten years—from 1936 to 1947—to complete the work. Hale did not live to see the 200-inch telescope completed. However, astronomers such as Hubble used it to help realize his vision.

In the meantime Hubble and Grace visited Mount Palomar, about ninety miles from

Pasadena. They drove along the Pacific Ocean then up through rolling mountains covered in live oaks and pines. They saw crews building roads to the top of the mountain where the gigantic telescope would one day stand. Over the months they saw the observatory's dome rise like a huge silver ball on Mount Palomar. When completed, the new observatory would need a director.

Although Hubble worked hard, he took time to relax. His favorite leisure time sport was fly-fishing for trout. He and Grace also traveled to England and Europe. There, they met not only important scientists, but also rich and famous artists, writers, musicians, and actors.

In 1936 he published *The Realm of the Nebulae*, telling the story of his work from 1922–1936. Though he did not have the powerful telescopes or computers that we have today, his work has stood the test of time. Scientists said that Hubble was a giant among them: "We stand on the shoulders of giants who have preceded us, and not one looms larger than Edwin Hubble."[1] Hubble was awarded the Bruce Gold Medal by the Astronomical Society of the Pacific, the Franklin Medal from Philadelphia's Franklin

Edwin Hubble, middle row center, with the rest of the staff of Wilson Observatory, outside of the Santa Barbara Street office.

Institute, and the Royal Astronomical Society's Gold Medal for 1940.

In 1938 Hubble was elected to the board of the Huntington Library and Art Gallery. The Hubbles enjoyed walking through the beautiful botanical gardens at Huntington. Their peaceful life together would be halted by World War II. World War I had changed Hubble's life. Now World War II (1939–1945) would again redirect his path.

World War II

By 1941 Adolph Hitler's German army had already defeated Belgium, Holland, France, and Eastern Europe. Now Germany and Britain were locked in a deadly war. Edwin began a crusade to get America into the war.[2] Those against America's entering the war attacked Hubble. He got phone calls and letters criticizing him for his stand, but he continued to speak out. Although Hubble was now too old to join the Army as a soldier, he wanted to help serve his country. On December 7, 1941, the Japanese bombed the American fleet at Pearl Harbor, and America entered the war.

In April 1942 Hubble was asked to travel to Maryland's Aberdeen Proving Grounds. A director of ballistics was needed. Ballistics is the study of the flight path of bullets, bombs, and rockets. Hubble's work in following the stars could now be applied to following the path of missiles. Hubble accepted the job because he understood that soldiers needed to know that firearms would accurately hit a target.

Many new firearms were being used for the first time, and no one had worked out exact firing tables for them. For example, how many miles

After the outbreak of World War II, Edwin Hubble was asked to become Chief of Ballistics at the Aberdeen Proving Grounds. Hubble's work at Aberdeen led to the development of more accurate weapons that helped soldiers on the battlefield.

away from its target should a bomb be released from a fast-moving plane? No one was even sure of the flight path of a rocket launched from the tail of a bomber. Hubble, with a team of scientists, had to work this out. Using high-speed movie cameras they photographed the path of a moving rocket launched from a plane. To get first-hand information about the firing of cannons and machine guns, he spent his days on the firing range. A Medal for Merit was presented to Hubble for his work as Chief of Ballistics at Aberdeen.

At first Grace stayed behind in California. She could not join her husband because they could find no place to stay near Aberdeen. A year later, however, they found a small, run-down cottage on an island in Chesapeake Bay, Maryland.

Hubble used the south side of the island to test top secret weapons. Often the cottage shook with the blasts from weapons being fired, and clouds of dust swirled around it. The Hubbles made the cottage their home until the end of the war in 1945. They even adopted a family of wild cats and a family of raccoons who lived in the cottage with them.

13

On Mount Palomar

WHILE HUBBLE HAD BEEN AWAY AT Aberdeen, his partner Milton Humason continued work on the redshift program with the 100-inch telescope. When Hubble returned he had just about finished this work. However, the 200-inch telescope at Mount Palomar was not yet completed. Until then, Hubble could not advance his work.

At this time Walter Adams, the director of Mount Wilson, was planning to retire. Hubble seemed to be the natural choice for the new director. But his fellow scientists were not so sure. They knew that he made a far better scientist than a director. They noted that over the years Hubble had failed to answer important business letters. He had not attended meetings of committees that he chaired. And he was often away from work on long trips to Britain and Europe. After careful thought they decided to give the directorship to a physics professor, Ira S. Bowen.

The news that he had been turned down as director shocked Hubble. After Hubble had time to think things over he was able to come to terms with the decision.

A New Cause

After the war Hubble took up a new cause. He spoke out against the use of atomic weapons. At Aberdeen, Hubble had seen the destruction caused by weapons of war. In 1945, to put an end to the war, America dropped the first atomic bombs on Japan. Thousands were killed, burned, or poisoned by nuclear radiation. Convinced that atomic weapons must be outlawed, he gave public speeches to warn people about the terrible danger of atomic warfare. He told a news reporter, "We live in constant awareness of the almost unlimited capacity of technology to destroy the world—or cure it of its ills."[1]

Seeing to the Limits of Space

In the optical shop at Caltech, opticians polished the huge mirror of the 200-inch telescope while tourists, among them Hubble, watched behind glass walls. At last, in 1947, it was ready to be transported to Mount Palomar Observatory. A sixteen-wheel diesel truck guarded by a highway patrol moved the mirror up the mountain. Once inside the dome, the lens was lowered into a vacuum chamber and coated with aluminum.

On June 3, 1948, the observatory was opened with a special ceremony. The telescope would act as a fine precision star camera with a million times the power of the human eye.[2] As heavy as a battleship and as tall as a ten-story tower, the telescope weighed five hundred tons.

At last Hubble could continue his quest to find answers to questions that have puzzled people since ancient times. What is the universe? How big is it? Is there a final boundary to space? He and Humason had measured galaxies about 50 million light-years away. Now they could measure objects 1 billion light-years away. Now they could see twice as far into space, maybe to its limits.

Hubble, now nearing sixty, hoped that he might win the Nobel Prize. He hired an agent to drum up publicity about his achievements. Photographs and articles about Hubble began to appear in newspapers and magazines. His name became even more widely known.

The Hubbles decided to take a trip to England in 1949. As they had done many times before, they crossed the Atlantic on an ocean liner. Upon reaching London they were shocked to see how badly the bombing had damaged the city. They then traveled to Switzerland.

When he returned to Palomar, Hubble wanted to start a new project. He wanted to make a more accurate count of the nebulae or galaxies than he had made in the 1930s. A new telescope, the 48-inch Schmidt, also at Palomar, made this possible. The Schmidt telescope had a much weaker light-collecting capability than the Hale. It could see only one third as far away as the Hale, but it was fitted with a special wide-angle lens that could photograph an area of the sky one thousand times as large.

Hubble hired Allan Sandage, a student at Caltech, to help with this painstaking project. Through the summer Sandage sat, straining his eyes, counting the number of galaxies observed on the photographic plates. Meanwhile Hubble was

Hubble gazes into the 48-inch telescope at the Mount Palomar Observatory. This telescope was fitted with a special wide-angle lens that made it easier for Hubble to make accurate counts of galaxies.

away on a fishing trip at his favorite Colorado ranch high in the mountains.

Health Problems Arise

One night he had sharp pains in his chest, but said nothing to Grace. By morning the pain was still there, and he asked her to call his doctor in California. When he described his symptoms, the doctor knew that Hubble was having a heart attack, and could die at any moment. Friends drove him down a steep mountain road to the nearest hospital several hours away.

Hubble stayed at the hospital with Grace at his side. The danger of another heart attack did not pass for several weeks. When news that the famous astronomer was ill got out, friends sent letters to cheer him. Grace, however, did not want the public to know how serious his illness was. When he finally became stronger, they took the train back home to California. His doctor accompanied him in case of an emergency. At home he rested for two months before returning to work.

14

The Quest Continues

FOUR MONTHS AFTER THE HEART ATTACK,
Hubble returned to work at his office. However, he
could never again work at the observatory in
winter. The thin cold mountain air was too
dangerous to his weakened heart. He would need
an assistant to continue his projects. Hubble
thought that Allan Sandage would do, but first he
put him to the test. Sandage had to learn to use the
60-inch telescope, a difficult instrument to operate.

While Sandage continued working on the
project, Grace and Hubble traveled to New York.
Then they toured France and England. When he
returned from his trip, Hubble's doctor said that
he could start working on Mount Palomar again.

He began three nights of work at the
observatory. On doctor's orders, Hubble put on a
heated suit to keep warm. Once inside the vast
dome, the scientists separated to their posts.

Sandage seated himself at the control panel on the main floor. Hubble began the ascent to the observation station high up in the throat of the giant telescope.[1]

He climbed the stairs, took an elevator, walked across a ramp, and got into a metal basket. A click of the controls hoisted him to a small steel cage suspended inside the telescope. Through the night he concentrated on taking the best plates possible.

At dawn, stiff from sitting in the small cage, Hubble took the elevator down. In the darkroom he developed his plates and left them to dry. Finally he could catch up on some sleep.

As a next step Hubble wanted to observe and count even more distant nebulae. Many hours of observing time would be needed to make this count. Yet Humason's work on the redshift project already used most of their observing time. As in the past, Hubble had to compete with other astronomers for use of the telescope. Hubble knew, however, that time might be running out for him.[2]

Last Honors

New honors came to Hubble. He received an honorary doctorate from the University of California at Berkeley. Universities and scientific

Hubble with his fishing gear, during one of his vacations to Rio Blanco, Colorado. Trout fishing is said to have been Hubble's favorite hobby.

societies invited him to give lectures. In 1953 he and Grace crossed the Atlantic to England aboard a luxury ocean liner. Though they did not know it, this would be their final crossing together.

Back in Pasadena, Hubble spent two nights at Mount Palomar. He told Grace that he would complete the redshift program in two years, but he would not live long enough to solve the other problems. Even with the 200-inch Hubble never reached the limits of the galaxies out in space.

A few weeks later, on September 28, on her way home, Grace saw Hubble walking along the street and stopped to pick him up. She noticed that he seemed strangely quiet. She asked if something was wrong, and he told her not to stop, but to drive home. By the time they drove up to the house he had died of a blood clot in his head.

According to his wishes, Grace had Hubble cremated. Only a few close friends saw his ashes buried in a secret place. When Grace died many years later, at the age of ninety, she too had her ashes buried in this secret place.

Hubble's Gift

After Hubble's death, Grace asked Sandage to complete *Hubble's Atlas of the Galaxies.* Sandage used Hubble's outstanding collection of plates taken between 1919 and 1948 to compile the atlas. Though Hubble died before he could complete his projects, his contributions to astronomy still stand. In his book *Realm of the Nebulae*, Hubble wrote that our knowledge fades rapidly as we search deeper in space. Still the search for knowledge will continue. That quest is Hubble's gift to modern astronomy.

Epilogue

ON APRIL 24, 1990, THE HUBBLE SPACE Telescope rocketed into space. This instrument, the size of a truck, circles 380 miles above the earth. It will search for the outer edges of the universe, perhaps to the beginning of the creation of the universe, the Big Bang.

The Hubble sends information to astronomers on earth. Powerful computers help them analyze and store that data. They are getting the first look at the universe from a telescope above earth's atmosphere. These images of planets, stars, and galaxies are twenty times sharper than those made by earth-based telescopes, which are blurred by the earth's atmosphere.

Astronomers lobbied to have the space telescope named after Edwin Hubble, because with it they can continue his quest. When asked what he expected to find with the 200-inch Mount

An astronaut performs maintenance on the Hubble Space Telescope during a space walk on February 15, 1997.

Palomar telescope in 1948, Hubble answered, "We hope to find something we hadn't expected."

The Hubble Space Telescope has found new and surprising information about the universe. As of this writing a key project of the Hubble Space Telescope is to find an accurate value of the Hubble Constant or H_0. It is one of the most important numbers because it is needed to estimate the size and age of the universe. Information from the telescope suggests that the universe may be younger than the oldest stars. Since this is impossible, scientists know that something is wrong with their current understanding of the universe. At the present time this is "the great debate." In time astronomers will solve some of these mysteries, only to begin new debates. Perhaps the next Edwin Hubble is reading this book and will discover the answers.

Activities

EXPLORE THE UNIVERSE WITH HUBBLE

Edwin Hubble was always asking questions about the universe. He listened to answers given by other scientists. He observed the night sky. Then he found new answers for himself. By training your mind to ask questions, you can explore the universe as he once did.

Activity 1: MAKE A SOAP BUBBLE UNIVERSE

Hubble proved that the universe is made up of thousands of galaxies. Go outside and blow many soap bubbles into the air. Now imagine that each bubble is a galaxy. Notice that each one is a different size, made up of soap film and empty space. If you could look at the entire universe from a great distance it would look like these soap bubbles.

Activity 2: BLOW UP THE UNIVERSE

Hubble discovered that the farther away a galaxy is, the faster it seems to be moving away from us. The galaxies seem to be rushing away as the universe expands. Try this experiment to get an idea of how this expansion works. Partly blow up a balloon. Then use a marking pen to make about twenty dots on it. Imagine the dots as galaxies, and the surface of the balloon as the universe. Now stand in front of a mirror and blow up the balloon. You will see that the dot galaxies move away from each other as the universe (your balloon) expands.

Activity 3: A TELESCOPE TIME MACHINE

Telescopes are really time machines that view the universe backward in time. Imagine that you are taking a trip in a telescope time machine. You are going to look at the Andromeda galaxy, 2.2 million light-years away from earth. That means that you are seeing light that has taken 2.2 million years to reach you. Therefore, you will see Andromeda as it was 2.2 million years ago.

Now get out your calculator and figure out how far one light-year is from earth. Remember, in the universe distance is measured by time. The speed light travels is 186,000 miles (299,792 kilometers) per second. In one minute, it travels 11,160,000 miles (or 186,000 × 60). In an hour that light will have traveled

In terms of astronomy, telescopes can be seen as visual time machines.

669,600,000 miles (1,079,251,200 kilometers). How far is a light-year? Multiply this last figure by the number of hours in a day and days in a year (669,600,000 × 24 × 365.25) and you will find out.

Chronology

1889—Born in Marshfield, Missouri, on November 20 to John Powell Hubble and Virginia Lee James.

1906—Graduated from high school and entered the University of Chicago.

1910—Graduated from the University.

1910–13—Rhodes Scholarship at Queen's College, Oxford University, in England.

1914—Graduate student in astronomy at the University of Chicago and assistant at Yerkes Observatory.

1916–17—Published first scientific paper; completed Ph.D. in astronomy.

1917–19—Served in the American Armed Forces during World War I.

1919—Began working at the Mount Wilson Observatory.

1922—Published a paper on the study of diffuse nebulae in the galaxy.

1922–26—Worked out a classification system for galaxies.

1923—Discovered a Cepheid variable in the Andromeda nebula; measured the distance to that galaxy, showing that it was outside the Milky Way.

1924—Received the American Association Prize for his paper "Cepheids in Spiral Nebulae"; married Grace Burke Leib.

1926–29—Published the results of his study of the Andromeda nebula; demonstrated proof of the island universe theory.

1927—Elected to the National Academy of Science of the United States.

1928—Elected to the Royal Astronomical Society of Britain.

1929—Demonstrated the law of redshift (Hubble's law).

1931–34—Together with Milton Humason proved Hubble's law.

1934—Published "The Distribution of Extra-Galactic Nebulae."

1935—Received honorary degree of Doctor of Science from Oxford; received the Barnard medal from Columbia University.

1936—Published the book *The Realm of the Nebulae*.

1938—Awarded the Bruce Gold Medal of the Astronomical Society of the Pacific.

1939—Awarded the Franklin Medal of the Franklin Institute.

1940—Awarded the Gold Medal of the Royal Astronomical Society of Great Britain; made public speeches calling for support of Britain in the war against Hilter's Germany.

1942–45—Director of the Ballistic Research Laboratory of the Aberdeen Proving Ground, Maryland.

1946—Received the Medal for Merit for his outstanding contribution to ballistic research during World War II.

1947—Elected to the Vienna Academy of Sciences.

1949—Made the first photographic plates with the 200-inch reflector of the Mount Palomar Observatory.

1953—Together with Allan Sandage published a scientific paper on variable stars in galaxies.

1953—Died of a stroke on September 28.

Chapter Notes

Introduction: Hubble's Quest

1. Milton L. Humason, "Edwin Hubble," *Monthly Notices of the Royal Astronomical Society*, 114, no. 3, 1954, p. 291.

2. John Kord Lagemann, "The Men of Palomar," *Collier's*, May 1949, p. 66.

3. Gale E. Christianson, *Edwin Hubble: Mariner of the Nebulae* (New York: Farrar, Straus and Giroux, 1995), pp. 112–136.

Chapter 1: School Days

1. Gale E. Christianson, *Edwin Hubble: Mariner of the Nebulae* (New York: Farrar, Straus and Giroux, 1995), p. 16.

2. N. U. Mayall, "Biographical Memoirs," *N.A.S.*, 41, 1970, p. 175.

3. Christianson, p. 18.

4. Donald E. Osterbrock, Ronald S. Brashear, and Joel A. Gwinn, "Self-Made Cosmologists: The Education of Edwin Hubble," published in *The Evolution of the Universe of Galaxies: Edwin Hubble*

Centennial Symposium (Vol. 10), edited by Richard G. Kron, San Francisco: the Astronomical Society of the Pacific, 1990, p. 2.

5. Christianson, pp. 25, 229.

6. Ibid., p. 30.

7. Ibid., p. 35.

Chapter 2: College Years

1. Gale E. Christianson, *Edwin Hubble: Mariner of the Nebulae* (New York: Farrar, Straus and Giroux, 1995), p. 38.

2. Ibid., p. 40.

3. Joel Gwinn, "Edwin Hubble in Louisville, 1913–1914," *The Filson Club Quarterly*, 1982, p. 415.

4. Christianson, p. 50.

5. Edwin P. Hubble to Martin Jones Hubble, August 24, 1909. In the Edwin P. Hubble Manuscript Collection, Henry Huntington Library, San Marino, California.

6. Donald E. Osterbrock, Ronald S. Brashear, and Joel A. Gwinn, "Self-Made Cosmologists: The Education of Edwin Hubble," published in *The Evolution of the Universe of Galaxies: Edwin Hubble Centennial Symposium* (Vol. 10), edited by Richard

G. Kron, San Francisco: the Astronomical Society of the Pacific, 1990, p. 4.

Chapter 3: **Queen's College, Oxford**

1. Donald E. Osterbrock, Ronald S. Brashear, and Joel A. Gwinn, "Self- Made Cosmologists: The Education of Edwin Hubble," published in *The Evolution of the Universe of Galaxies: Edwin Hubble Centennial Symposium* (Vol. 10), edited by Richard G. Kron, San Francisco: the Astronomical Society of the Pacific, 1990, p. 4.

2. Ibid.

3. Gale E. Christianson, *Edwin Hubble: Mariner of the Nebulae* (New York: Farrar, Straus and Giroux, 1995), p. 65.

4. Ibid., p. 67.

5. Osterbrock, Brashear, and Gwinn, p. 5.

Chapter 4: **The Yerkes Observatory**

1. Donald E. Osterbrock, Ronald S. Brashear, and Joel A. Gwinn, "Self-Made Cosmologists: The Education of Edwin Hubble," published in *The Evolution of the Universe of Galaxies: Edwin Hubble Centennial Symposium* (Vol. 10), edited by Richard G. Kron, San Francisco: the Astronomical Society of the Pacific, 1990, p. 5.

2. Ibid.

3. Gale E. Christianson, *Edwin Hubble: Mariner of the Nebulae* (New York: Farrar, Straus and Giroux, 1995), p. 86.

4. Ibid., p. 87.

5. N. U. Mayall, "Biographical Memoirs," *N.A.S.*, 41, 1970, 175, p. 1.

6. Astronomers use special systems for identifying and naming different nebulae and stars. One system is the New General Catalog or NGC. This catalog was published by the Irish astronomer John L. Dreyer in 1888.

Chapter 5: Off to War!

1. Donald Osterbrock, "The California-Wisconsin Axis in American Astronomy," *Sky and Telescope*, January 1976, p. 11.

2. Brian Jones, "The Legacy of Edwin Hubble," *Astronomy*, 17, no. 12, December 1989, p. 40.

3. Directors Papers, Yerkes Observatory Archives, Yerkes Observatory, Williams Bay, Wisconsin.

4. Donald E. Osterbrock, Ronald S. Brashear, and Joel A. Gwinn, "Self-Made Cosmologists: The Education of Edwin Hubble," published in *The Evolution of the Universe of Galaxies: Edwin Hubble*

Centennial Symposium (Vol. 10), edited by Richard G. Kron, San Francisco: the Astronomical Society of the Pacific, 1990, p. 7.

5. Ibid.

6. Gale E. Christianson, *Edwin Hubble: Mariner of the Nebulae* (New York: Farrar, Straus and Giroux, 1995), p. 107.

7. Ibid., p. 109.

Chapter 6: Mount Wilson

1. Gale E. Christianson, *Edwin Hubble: Mariner of the Nebulae* (New York: Farrar, Straus and Giroux, 1995), p. 125.

2. Michael Simmons, "The History of Mount Wilson Observatory: Bringing Astronomy to an Isolated Mountaintop," *Mount Wilson Observatory Association*, 1983, <http://www.mtwilson.edu/History> (June 28, 2006).

3. Christianson, p. 119.

4. Ibid., p. 118.

Chapter 7: The Great Debate

1. Gale E. Christianson, *Edwin Hubble Mariner of the Nebulae* (New York: Farrar, Straus and Giroux, 1995), p. 140.

2. Edwin Hubble, "The Exploration of Space," *Sky and Telescope*, May 1960, p. 400.

3. Christianson, p. 135.

4. Otto Struve, "A Historic Debate About the Universe," *Sky and Telescope*, May 1960, pp. 398–401.

Chapter 8: In Depths of Space

1. Alexander S. Sharkov and Igor D. Novikov, *Edwin Hubble the Discoverer of the Big Bang Universe* (New York: Cambridge University Press, 1983), p. 17.

2. The number M31 is from Charles Messier's great catalogue (list) of nebulae, <http://www.seds.org/messier/xtra/history/biograph.html> (June 28, 2006).

3. Hubble did not like to use the term *galaxy* to describe the stellar systems beyond our Milky Way. He used the term *nebula* rather than *galaxy*, <http://www.pbs.org/wnet/hawking/cosmostar/html/cstars_hubble.html> (June 28, 2006).

4. Sharkov and Novikov, p. 31.

5. Gale E. Christianson, *Edwin Hubble Mariner of the Nebulae* (New York: Farrar, Straus and Giroux, 1995), pp. 232–233.

6. Ibid., p. 166.

7. Donald E. Osterbrock, Ronald S. Brashear, and Joel A. Gwinn, "Self-Made Cosmologists: The

Education of Edwin Hubble," published in *The Evolution of the Universe of Galaxies: Edwin Hubble Centennial Symposium* (Vol. 10), edited by Richard G. Kron, San Francisco: the Astronomical Society of the Pacific, 1990, p. 1.

Chapter 9: Classification of Galaxies

1. Gale E. Christianson, *Edwin Hubble: Mariner of the Nebulae* (New York: Farrar, Straus and Giroux, 1995), p. 172.

Chapter 10: The Big Bang

1. Slipher showed that the lines shifted toward the violet end of the spectrum. He therefore reasoned that the Andromeda galaxy was coming toward us. This is an exception because Andromeda is a very close member of the local group of galaxies. <http://www.roe.ac.uk/~jap/slipher/> (June 28, 2006).

2. John Kord Lagemann, "The Men of Palomar," *Collier's*, May 1949, p. 66.

3. Brian Denis, *Einstein: A Life* (New York: John Wiley and Sons, Inc., 1996), p. 213.

Chapter 11: Fame and Fortune

1. Brian Denis, *Einstein: A Life* (New York: John Wiley and Sons, Inc., 1996), p. 213.

2. Donald E. Osterbrock, Ronald S. Brashear, and Joel A. Gwinn, "Self-Made Cosmologists: The Education of Edwin Hubble," published in *The Evolution of the Universe of Galaxies: Edwin Hubble Centennial Symposium* (Vol. 10), edited by Richard G. Kron, San Francisco: the Astronomical Society of the Pacific, 1990, p. 1.

3. Gale E. Christianson, *Edwin Hubble: Mariner of the Nebulae* (New York: Farrar, Straus and Giroux, 1995), p. 220.

4. Ibid., p. 221.

5. Ibid., p. 223.

Chapter 12: The Realm of the Nebulae

1. Edwin Hubble, *Realm of the Nebulae* (New Haven: Yale University Press, 1936), p. xvi.

2. Alexander S. Sharkov and Igor D. Novikov, *Edwin Hubble the Discoverer of the Big Bang Universe* (New York: Cambridge University Press, 1983), p. 91.

Chapter 13: On Mount Palomar

1. Gordon L'Allemand, "Pilgrimage Into Eternity," *Travel*, September 1949, pp. 21–25.

2. David O. Woodbury, "Behold the Universe," *Collier's*, May 1949, pp. 20–22.

Chapter 14: **The Quest Continues**

1. John Kord Lagemann, "The Men of Palomar," *Collier's*, May 1949, p. 64.

2. Gale E. Christianson, *Edwin Hubble: Mariner of the Nebulae* (New York: Farrar, Straus and Giroux, 1995), p. 345.

Glossary

Andromeda galaxy—Major spiral galaxy, 2.2 million light-years from Earth. It is approaching us; most other galaxies are moving away from us.

Big Bang theory—This theory states that the universe began as very hot and dense matter that cooled as the universe expanded.

constellation—Groups of stars that were named for the shape that they were imagined to form, such as Cancer the crab. There are eighty-eight constellations.

Doppler effect—Change in the wavelength of light or sound given off by a moving body. Absorption lines in the spectrum will be shifted toward the red end. The relation between the redshift of light from the galaxies and their distance is important evidence for the expansion of the universe. (See Big Bang theory.)

Einstein's general theory of relativity—Theory of gravity that predicts the universe is expanding.

expansion of the universe—Constant increase over time in the distance between galaxies. Expansion does not take place within individual galaxies because they are held together by their gravitational pull.

galaxy—A system of gas and millions of stars. There are three major classifications of galaxies—spiral, elliptical, and irregular. Our sun belongs to a spiral galaxy, the Milky Way galaxy. There are billions of galaxies in our universe.

gravity—The attraction (or pull) of massive objects to one another. Gravity makes objects fall toward earth, and keeps earth revolving around the sun. Einstein's general relativity is a theory of gravity.

Hubble Constant (H_o)—The rate at which the universe expands, equal to about 50 kilometers per second of velocity (speed) per megaparsec of distance. Now, using the space telescopes, many observers believe it is 70 or 80 kilometers per second.

Hubble's law—The law states that distant galaxies are moving away from one another at speeds proportional to (matching) their distances using redshift-distance relationship.

interstellar space—The volume between stars.

island universe hypothesis—The idea that the spiral nebulae are other galaxies of stars.

light-year—The distance light travels in one year, about 6 trillion miles.

local groups—A group of galaxies to which the Milky Way and the Andromeda galaxies belong.

luminosity (L)—The energy radiated per second by a celestial body.

luminous energy (Q_v)—The total amount of light emitted by a source.

Magellanic Clouds—Two irregular galaxies that lie close to the Milky Way galaxy. They can be seen in the southern skies of Earth.

megaparsec—The units of the Hubble Constant are "kilometers per second per megaparsec." A parsec is equal to 3.26 light-years.

Milky Way galaxy—The spiral galaxy in which Earth's sun is found. It appears as a glowing band of light across the skies of earth. The light comes from stars and nebulae.

nebulae—Faint objects that can be seen in the night sky. "Bright" nebulae glow from the light of gas of which they are made, or from reflections from starlight. "Dark" nebulae are made of clouds of gas and dust. Spiral nebulae are really galaxies.

novae—Stars that suddenly increase in brightness for several days without warning.

redshift—Shifting of the spectral lines in light coming from the stars of distant galaxies, caused by these galaxies speeding outward in the expanding universe. The farther a galaxy, the faster it is receding from the earth.

redshift-distance relation—The proportionality (match) between redshift in the spectra of galaxies and their distance (see Hubble's law). To calculate H_0 astronomers use the velocity or speed of a galaxy and the galaxy's distance from the earth.

spectrograph—A device made of a prism that breaks up light into the colors of the rainbow. The spectrograph makes a photographic record of the spectrum.

spectrum—A record of the pattern of dark or bright lines versus the wavelength of light. Spectra can be studied to learn about the motion of stars and galaxies.

telescope—A tool for gathering light or other energy. Refracting telescopes gather light by means of a lens. Reflecting telescopes gather light by a mirror.

variable stars—A star that changes in brightness in a regular fashion. There are many types of variable stars. Cepheids are a class of bright variable stars with a very *regular* bright-to-dim cycle (or period). A well-known relationship between brightness and period makes Cepheids useful in measuring distances between objects in space.

Further Reading

Books

Christianson, Gale E. *Edwin Hubble: Mariner of the Nebulae*. Chicago: University of Chicago Press, 1997.

Fox, Mary Virginia. *Edwin Hubble: American Astronomer*. Danbury, Conn.: Franklin Watts, 1997.

MacDonald, Fiona. *Edwin Hubble*. Chicago: Heinemann Library, 2003.

Sharov, Alexander S., and Igor D. Novikov. *Edwin Hubble, The Discoverer of the Big Bang Universe*. Cambridge, Mass.: Cambridge University Press, 2005.

Zannos, Susan. *Edwin Hubble and the Theory of the Expanding Universe*. Bear, Del.: Mitchell Lane, 2003.

Internet Addresses

Edwin Hubble

http://www.edwinhubble.com/

Time 100: Edwin Hubble

http://www.time.com/time/time100/scientist/
profile/hubble03.html

**A Science Odyssey: People and Discoveries:
Edwin Hubble**

http://www.pbs.org/wgbh/aso/databank/entries/
bahubb.html

NASA—Hubble Space Telescope

http://www.nasa.gov/worldbook/hubble_telescope
_worldbook.html

Index